COLOURING BOOK

An Insight Editions Book

With her passion for justice, fearlessness in battle, and bold sense of style, Wonder Woman is one of the most iconic Super Heroes of all time. From her red-and-blue costume to her golden Lasso of Truth, vibrant colours have been essential to bringing her stories to life on the page.

Let the full-colour art from classic Wonder Woman comics featured at the end of this book serve as a guide and inspiration for creating your own exciting adventures with the ultimate Amazonian Super Hero.

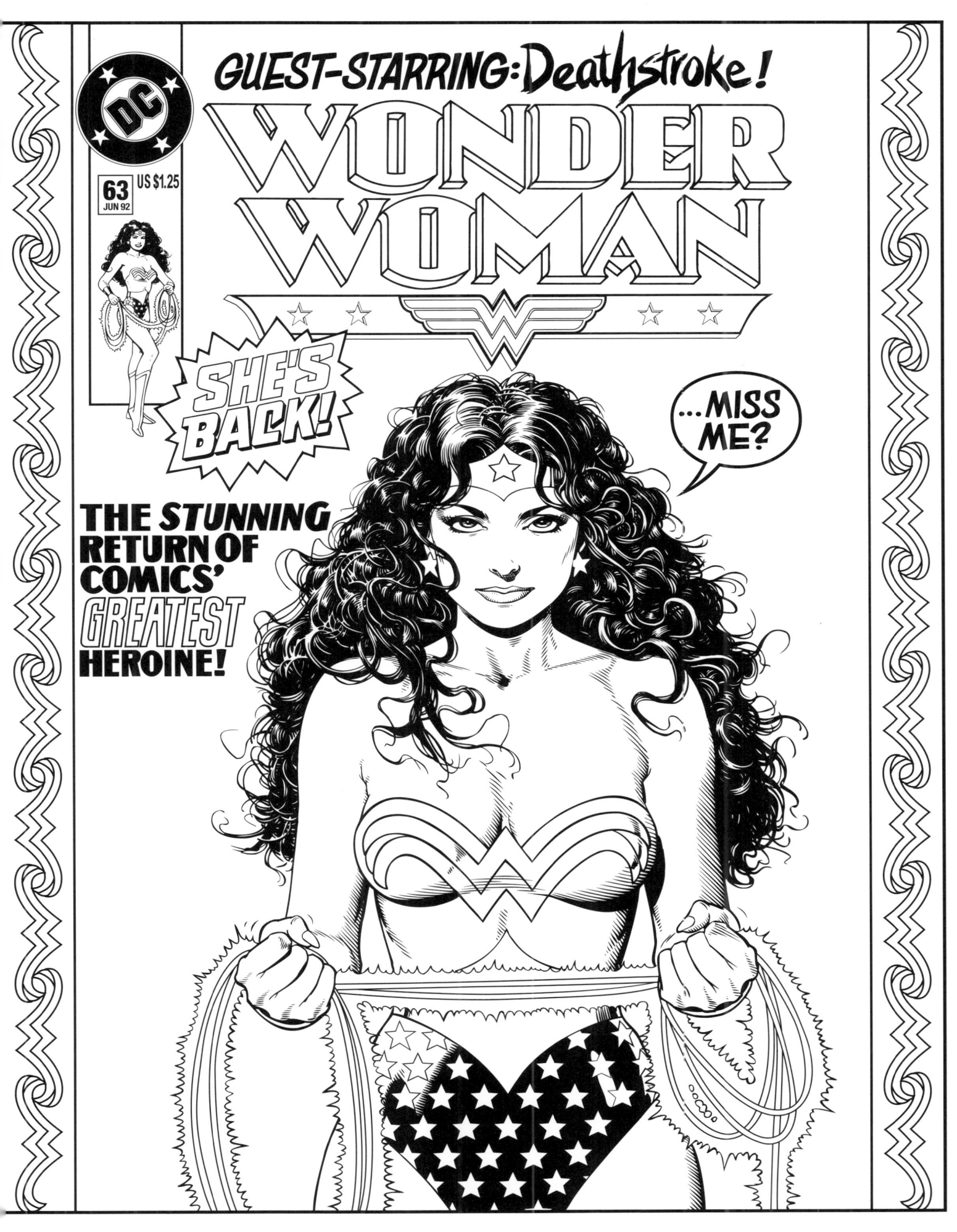

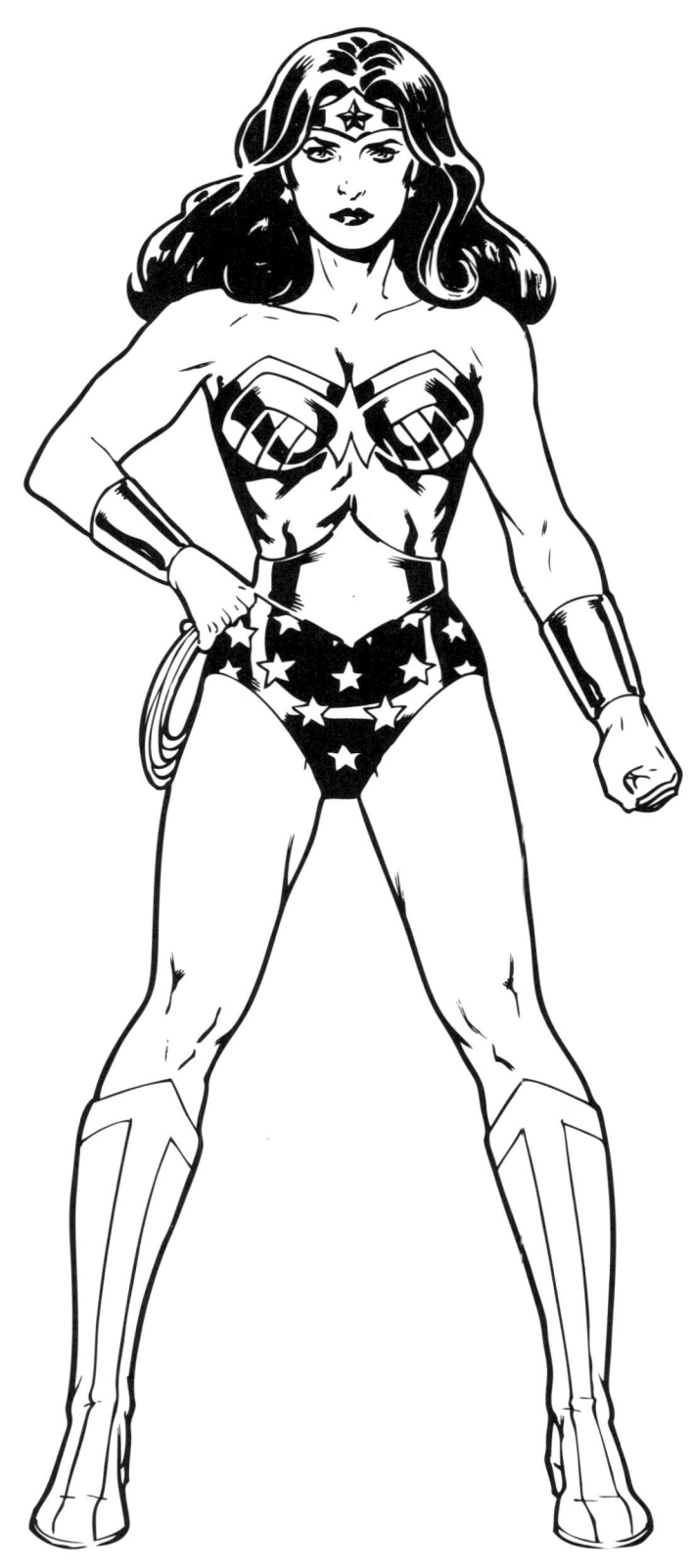

| HEROES UNITED | GLOBAL DEFENDERS | JUSTICE LEAGUE | TEAM POWER |

| HEROES UNITED | GLOBAL DEFENDERS | JUSTICE LEAGUE | TEAM POWER |

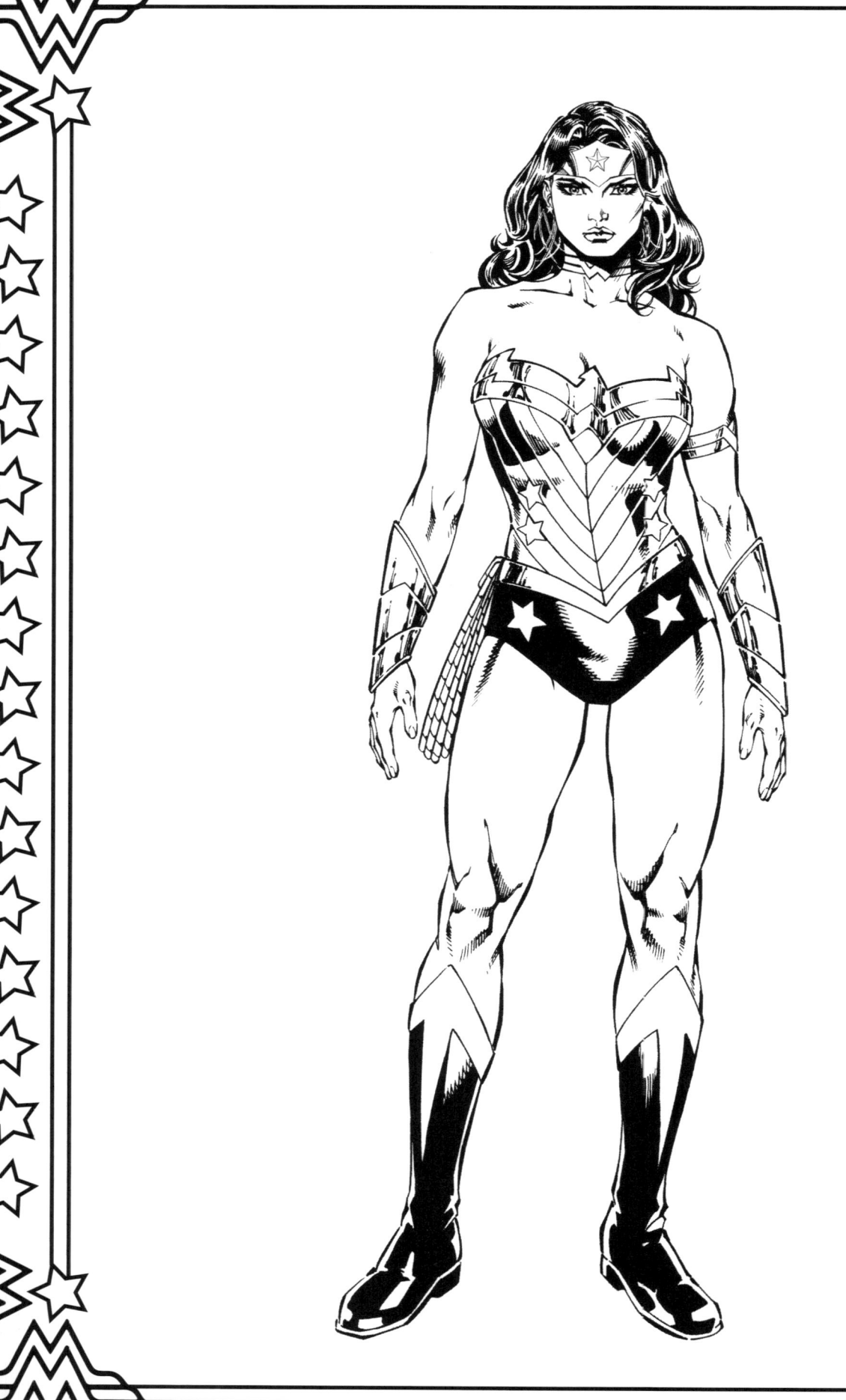

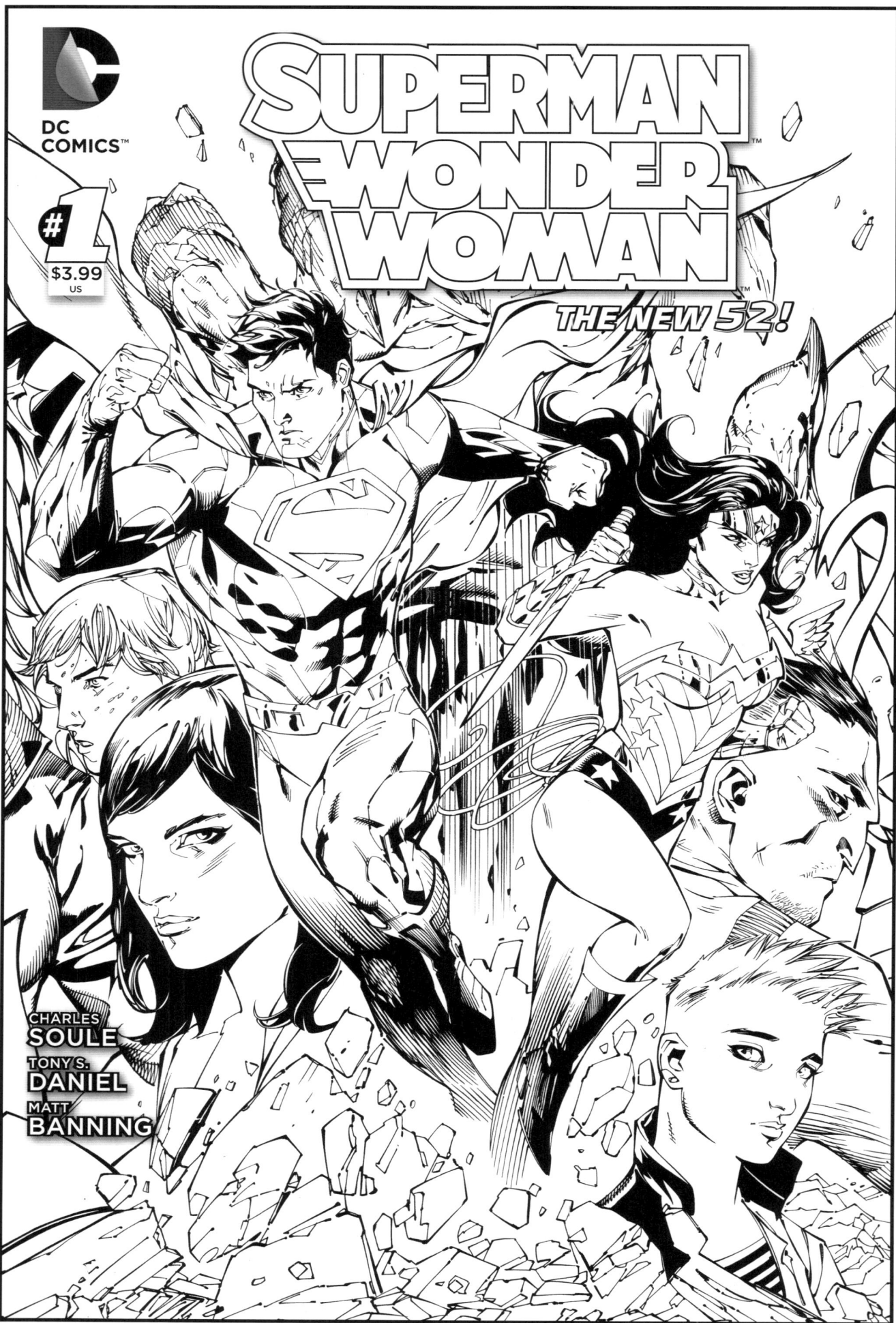

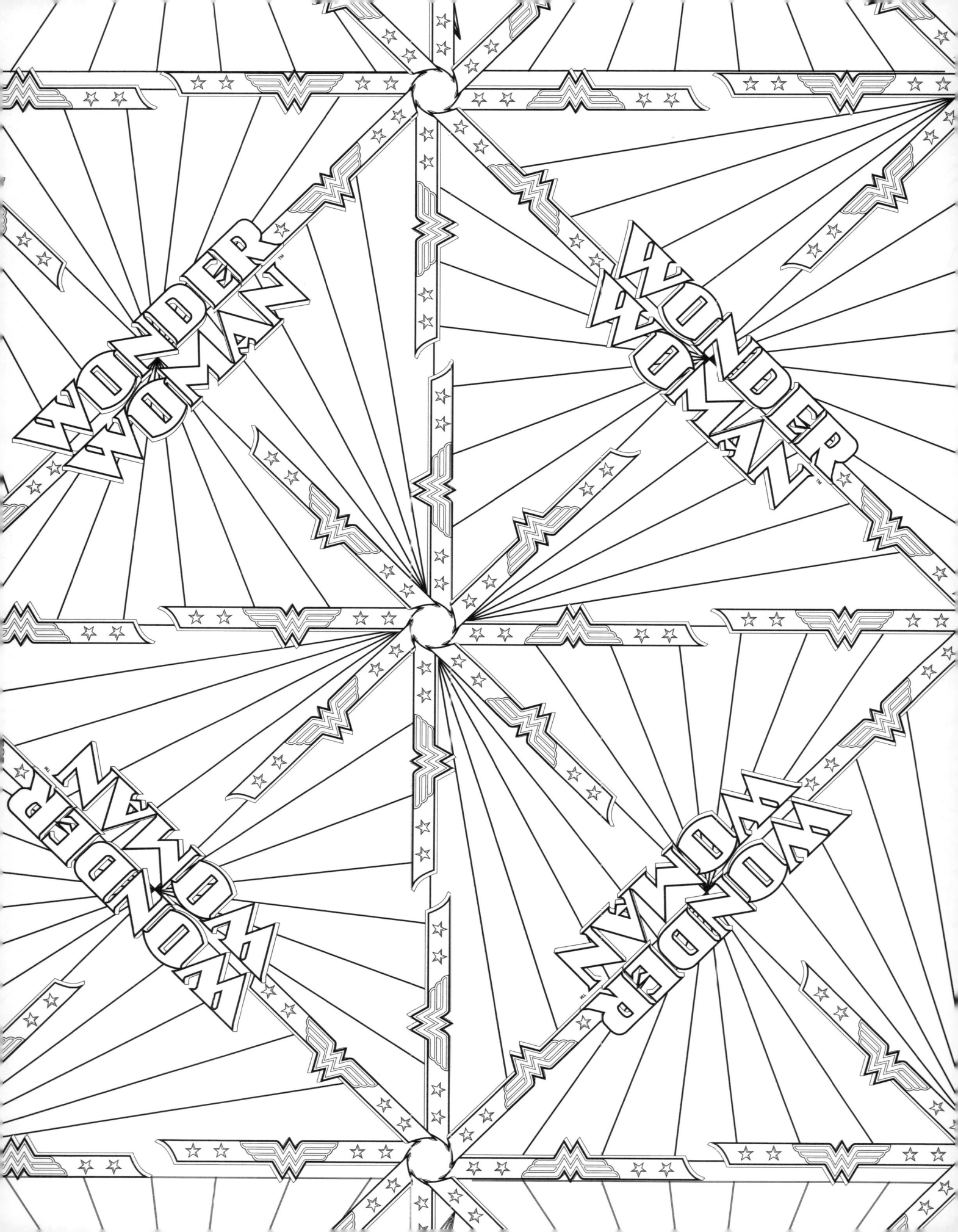

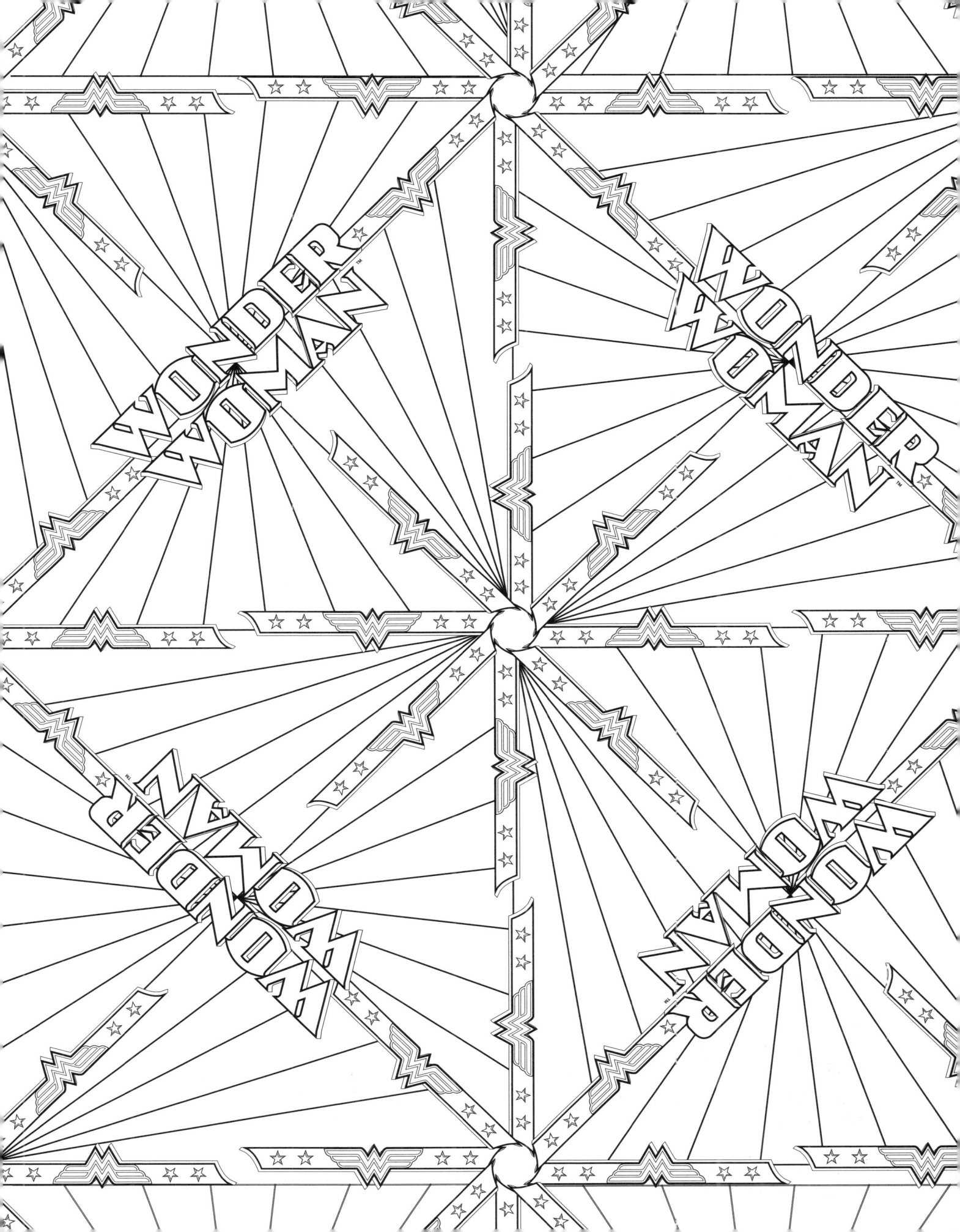

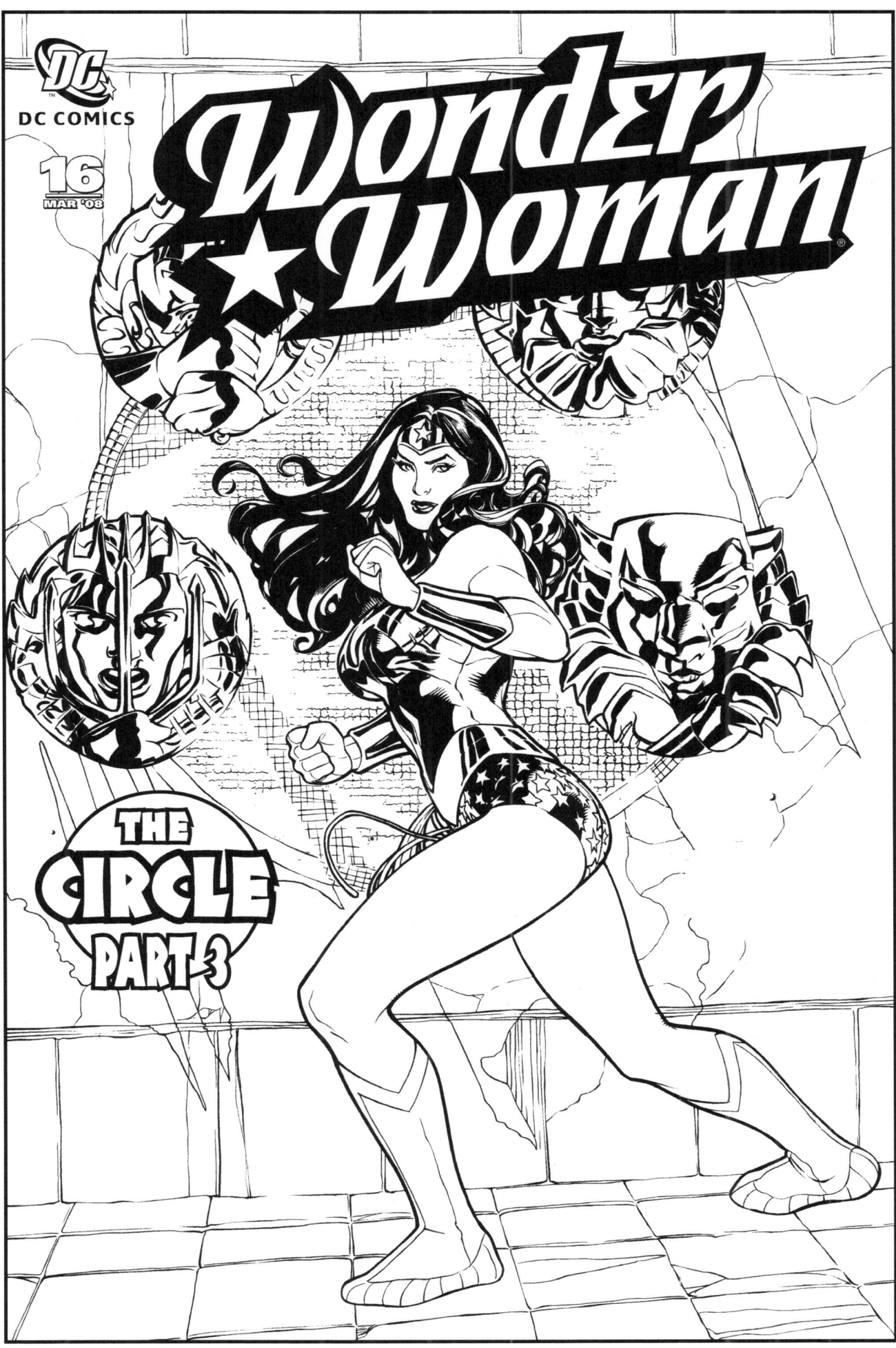

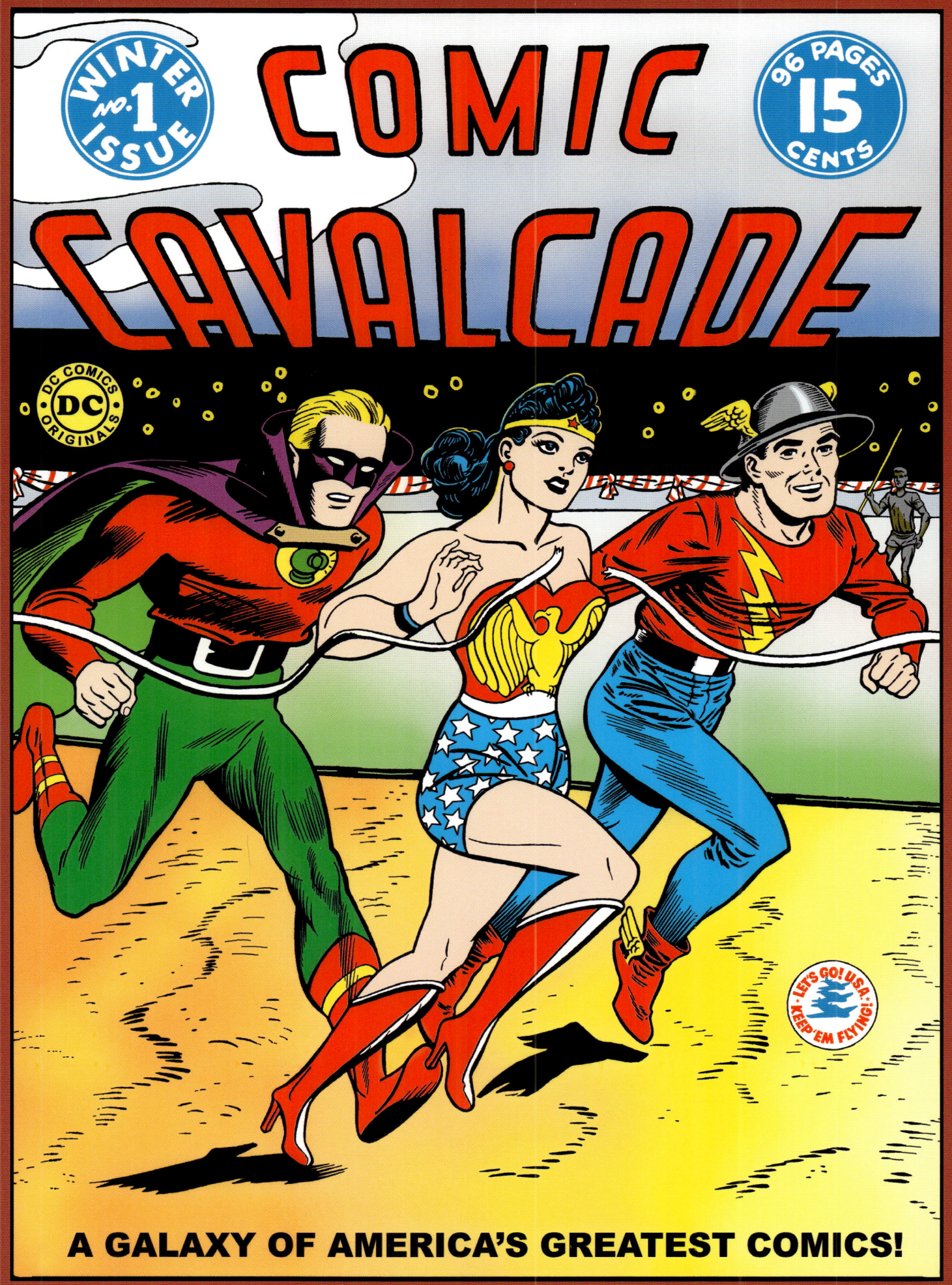

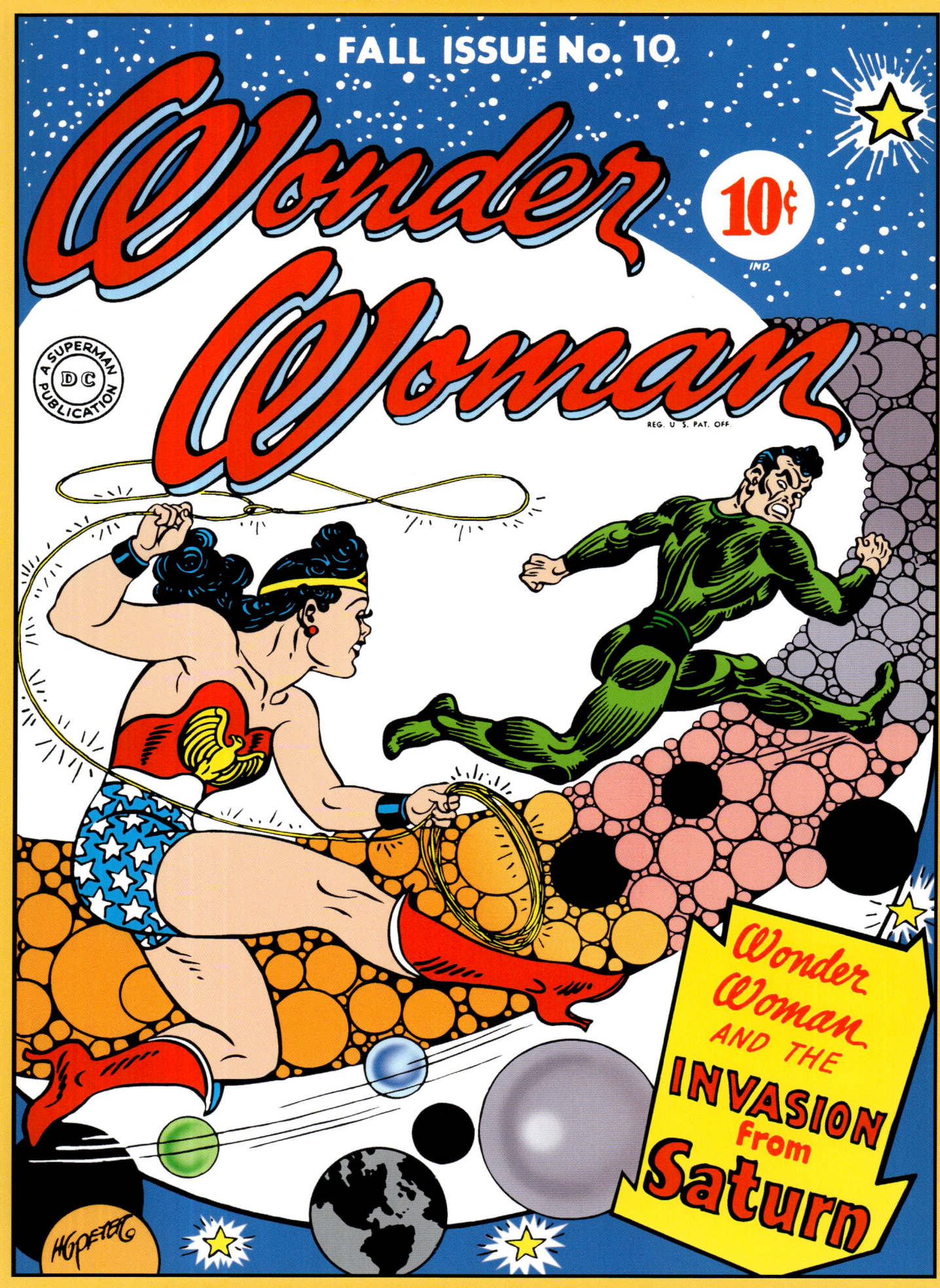

INSIGHT EDITIONS
PO Box 3088
San Rafael, CA 94912
www.insighteditions.com

Copyright © 2016 DC Comics.
WONDER WOMAN and all related characters and elements are © and ™ DC Comics.
DC LOGO: ™ & © DC Comics.
WB SHIELD: ™ & © WBEI. (s16)

Wonder Woman created by William Moulton Marston.

All rights reserved.

Published under license by Studio Press, an imprint of Kings Road Publishing,
part of the Bonnier Publishing Group.

The publisher does not have any control over and does not assume any responsibility
for author or third-party websites or their content.

No part of this publication may be reproduced, stored in a retrieval system, or transmitted in
any form, or by any means electronic, mechanical, photocopying, recording, or otherwise,
without written permission of the publisher. For information regarding permission, write to
Studio Press, The Plaza, 535 King's Road, London, SW10 0SZ.

ISBN: 978-1-78370-727-0

Publisher: Raoul Goff
Acquisitions Manager: Robbie Schmidt
Art Director: Chrissy Kwasnik
Designer: Malea Clark-Nicholson
Executive Editor: Vanessa Lopez
Project Editor: Kelly Reed
Production Editor: Elaine Ou
Associate Editor: Katie DeSandro
Production Manager: Carol Rough and Lina sp Temena
Production Assistant: Sam Taylor and Jacob Frink

ROOTS of PEACE   REPLANTED PAPER

Insight Editions, in association with Roots of Peace, will plant two trees for each tree used in the
manufacturing of this book. Roots of Peace is an internationally renowned humanitarian organization
dedicated to eradicating land mines worldwide and converting war-torn lands into productive farms
and wildlife habitats. Roots of Peace will plant two million fruit and nut trees in Afghanistan and
provide farmers there with the skills and support necessary for sustainable land use.

Manufactured in Italy by Insight Editions